FOREVER, NOW

Helen Cadbury (1965-2017) was a British crime fiction author, poet and playwright, whose debut novel *To Catch a Rabbit* won the Northern Crime Award, was an Amazon Rising Star, and was chosen as one of the Yorkshire Post's "top novels since the millennium to reflect the region". It was the first in an ongoing series featuring PCSO Sean Denton.

Helen was born in the Midlands, grew up in Saddleworth, near Oldham, and spent the last 15 years of her life in York. When she was a child she wanted to be an actor, a writer, or an ice cream man's assistant – with two out of three achieved, she said in May 2017: 'I'm still looking for an opening in the ice cream trade.' *Forever, Now* is the first collection of her poetry.

Forever, Now

HELEN CADBURY

Valley Press

First published in 2017 by Valley Press
Woodend, The Crescent, Scarborough, YO11 2PW
www.valleypressuk.com

First edition, first printing (November 2017)

ISBN 978-1-908853-94-3
Cat. no. VP0111

Cover photograph by the author.
Cover and text design by Jamie McGarry.

Printed and bound in England by SRP Ltd, Exeter.

Contents

Author's Acknowledgements

These poems have been published previously, as follows:

'Five Haiku' and 'On Burgess Street' were first published in *Staple*, no. 64. (2006) ed. Ann Atkinson and Elizabeth Barrett.

'Sestina For Rachel' appeared as a shortlisted poem in the *Arvon International Poetry Competition Anthology 2006*.

'Cat Brooch: A Gift From the British Museum'; 'Late'; and 'Collecting Reuben From School' were first published in *Sometimes*, Cinnamon Press, (2006) ed. Jan Fortune-Wood.

'Vestige' was originally published in *Mint Sauce*, Cinnamon Press, (2008) ed. Jan Fortune-Wood.

'From the Norse' was first published in *Matter 9*, Mews Press, (2009) ed. A.J. Ashworth.

'Functional Skills Maths' first appeared as a piece of visual art at Rotherham Open Arts Renaissance (ROAR) exhibition in 2015.

'Marking' first appeared in an exhibition, with a photograph by the author, at ROAR, April 2017.

'My Boy is Eighteen Today' was first published online on the *Writers For Calais Refugees* website (2015) curated by Marie Lightman.

'Fog' and 'The Axe Sings its Own Song' were first published online on *The Guardian Poetry Workshop* (2005, 2006).

I would like to thank Jo Haywood and Jamie McGarry for their belief, support and editorial oversight in bringing this collection together. I am honoured to be part of the Valley Press family of poets.

I would particularly like to thank Carole Bromley, for being there right from the beginning. She has inspired me and fired me up in my writing, believed in me and finally ensured that I had this legacy of work to share. She has been my teacher, mentor, but above all, my much loved friend.

for my family and friends, with all my love

British Library

If there really is a heaven, I think
it's like Humanities Reading Room Two,
full of light, knowledge, silence.

So pleased with that, I tweet it.

Researching the demise of Walthamstow
dog track, I wait for my books to come up
from the stack, and consider how rarely in novels,
and never in poems, does anyone go to the toilet,

while in the Ladies, the women come and go,
dimly lit, on floors of Portland stone.

Wandering to the exhibition on Floor One
I learn that Qikitarkil is an island on a lake
which isn't on the map. Innisfree comes
to mind instead: bean rows and long-dead bees.
I chart the Northwest Passage,
all that white, those ice-floes,
while voices mingle on the benches by the stairs

the thing is
        it's not like that in Spain
a definitive approach
                gegenfalls
which makes it
        she wore nail varnish like mustard
Inshallah

a hub of migration, like the bird reserve at Gibraltar Point.
So pleased with that, I reach for my phone

and drop my notebook. The young birds fly up
still chattering. A word is left on the floor

neb – from the Yorkshire: nose. Swedish: sharp beak.

Pecking around like a barnacle goose
looking for one thing, I've found another.
Upstairs, *Last Days at the Dogs* is waiting.

Primary, 2015

Like that time at Christmas,
playing out with my brothers,
aged nine or ten, it was the same then;
I didn't see it coming.

Only when my cheeks were stinging,
as heat follows cold, did I know
it was a snowball, thrown short-range,
over-arm, smack in the face,

the air in my lungs sucked out
like a fish, that moment before
the floundering begins, that struggle
for air, willing the tears to stay back.

II. MARKING

some people find this bit distressing.

The warning bounces off the carapace I've grown
ever since I've known what has to happen.

I don't look away, I watch him circle
my breast with his blue felt pen, a steady line.
Good, I think, for those hands will wield the knife,

and the needle to stitch me back together again.

III.   RECONSTRUCTION

At Roskilde we spent the day looking at ships
found in the fjord after a thousand years,
hulls full of stones, old boats dumped to protect the land.

We learned how archeologists hung
what was left on a frame, spars like ribs,
one side of the hull solid, the other full of air.

We touched the replicas, built from clues in the Sagas,
new cloth woven and stretched for sails, young oaks
cut for masts. But I preferred the old wrecks,

rope-scarred and waterlogged, whispering their history
in the spaces between curves of blackened wood
cut from a tree that had grown against the wind.

IV. SINCE YOU ASK

It's not quite
but almost like
a hangover.
Touch of flu.
The near-faint
that comes
from inexperienced
smoking.
The sense of being
off your head.
Morning sickness,
motion sickness,
drunk,
like someone's
spiked your drink.

Want to try it?

Thought not.

V. FIRST ANNUAL CHECK-UP

We talk books. He says he hated Austerlitz

        (long fingers feel their way across my chest)

He says his book group's too conservative

        (fingertips press into my armpits)

They won't read comedy or crime. He says

        it's fine, he's concentrating, honestly.

He hopes I'll find the time to write my book

        before we meet again next year.

There's nothing unexpected here today.

Self-Portrait

Chameleon
who gives
herself away
with one slip
of a hungry tongue.
It goes on
and on
unravelling.

The 8.45 a.m. Saturday Service

A perfect rainbow arcs over rooftops from Rotherham,
while four men compare real ales and talk about their mate
who knows after the seventh pint, the names of the six before,
and can still name that special beer he drank once in Accrington.

Across the aisle, advice about insomnia mingles with the price
of an umbrella, reduced because the woman's daughter's boyfriend
works in Next, and the trolley rattles past with a smile
from Fatima, on board since five o'clock from Waverley.

Outside, the carcass of a factory gapes open to the wind,
clouds back away and the end of the rainbow tips into Sheaf
    Square,
turns to fine rain, shines up the pavement and the shoes of a
    policeman,
who stands waiting for trouble to shuffle off a football train.

Isabel's *Tarantella*

In the artist's house, where apple blossom
smothers the window, I move on soft carpets
past each painting, until one canvas shouts
from the wall, claps its hands, stamps hard
on wooden boards, stirs up a blur of red dust.

Meanwhile, in the garden, a collared dove
is trapped in the greenhouse, wings fanned out,
beak like a castanet, body hitting the glass.

Postcards from York Minster

Sister Ignatia stands in the garden,
watching cherry blossom fall.
One petal turns, flies back.
She slaps it away
and sees it was a butterfly.

When Claude came as a boy,
lorries rumbled by, shaking
the bones of saints. Today,
his café chair rocks on paving,
knocks at the roof of their tombs.

Walking backwards in the courtyard
Mrs Yamahoto cannot take it in,
stone walls, gargoyles
and yellowing sky, like the two-day
bruise beneath her eye.

Shelter

You could be any man of a certain age,
shoulders hunched under greasy nylon,
but it's that scar, the silvery track ringing

your thumb, that gives you away before your voice
cracks the air, smoke-burned from a thousand
roll-ups, vodka binges, whisky nights and you,

hundreds of miles from home, still have Devon
hanging in your vowels, as you thank me,
without looking up, for a mug of sweet tea.

When the wound was fresh, the slip of a knife
in the sail-mending shed, jagged red,
and my tee shirt the only bandage,

your eyes pierced mine, bright as the sun
flashing off Seaton Bay, 'Careless Whisper'
on the radio as I held tight, raised your arm

to stop the flow, your mouth
against my shoulder, the rough skin
of your free palm like pumice on my back.

Trains

I wish that words could be as fast
as oil paint that's slicked on thick
with palette knife on sheets of glass,
the greens and fawns and twiggy browns
of fields and hedges rushing past.
The cooling towers and pylon brides
trail veils of live electric wires
to red-brick clumps of new-build homes.
But paint alone cannot contain
the symphony that plays inside,
a choir of piercing mobile phones,
vibrations trailing to a hum,
the muffled whine of wheel on track,
I wish that words could be as fast.

Vestige

n: trace – origin Latin: footprint

It came to her

    as she walked

        on herringbone pavia

            looking down

                she

  understood

           that a man had knelt

      and laid each brick

    tenderly

in an interlocking V

Cat Brooch: A Gift From the British Museum

i.m. Fritz Thorn

On a search for Fritz's cat
I enter a temple, dodge a god
who threatens to drop

a gold ball on a passing child.
I shrink to Lilliputian woman
next to supersize pillars

pass a blind lion whose eyes
were once filled with glass
flashing back the sunset in Asia Minor

and all the while Fritz's cat nests
on my chest, gold fur lying flat,
until we come across a body,

headless, armless, torso of a boy
bobbing in glass, head stuck crudely back
after it was found in a country house

along with stuffed animals
and mutilated naked men
suggesting an elite international plot.

Fritz's cat – copy of Baxter's engraving –
will have to wait,
Drawings and Prints closed until July.

Eve's Garden

When we had to leave,
we took it with us;
rolled up the grass, moss,
fallen leaves, half-eaten apples,

tucked the untrimmed edges
around remains of autumn
colchicums, moth-larvae, earwigs,
a deflated World Cup football,
spent fireworks, the bulging sack
of kitchen waste.

The blackbirds, hedge sparrows
and coal tits followed us at first,
but the place we found was harsher,
the wind blew from the East
and it was years before
there was enough to share.

My husband's hands grew hard,
his back wide.
My hips spread to carry children,
baskets, bundles of sticks.
The cold ground was good though.
No snakes.

Holy Marys in the Archive

On March 10th, a cloth-dresser
is brought from Leeds
to the Yorkshire Spring Assizes.

Guilty of assault on a female
infant child, under the age of ten,
with intent to carnally know and abuse her

a child of six, another of eight,
the age of the third has worn away
in the crease of the page.
Mary Clark, Mary Frankland, Mary Oddy.

John Holmes is imprisoned for five years.
Mary Holmes, his wife, discharged.

The same day, Mary Lazenby
is brought before the court.
Her baby died, but had it lived,
it would have been a bastard.

She's cleared of murder
but serves two months
for burying the body
in an ash-hole.

I light a candle to you, Marys,
beneath your namesake,
in her robe of blue glass,
her eyes turned away.

The Book of Ruth

1. NAOMI

I look at you, tears of mourning
still muddy on your cheeks, wonder at
your great tenacity. I give you warning;

I haven't much to offer. Nothing that
compares with what your youth deserves.
My husband's dead, sons too, who I begat

to fill a destiny, a line, preserve
the family name. I have no choice
but to return and serve

my widowhood in Bethlehem. The voice
of my own people calls. If you are by my side,
well, that's your choice.

II. RUTH

I wouldn't let you go alone, Naomi,
across the dust-blown tracks, where heat and thieves
await the vulnerable. You're more to me

in life, in law, than my own kin. I leave
my family with ease; they gave me once before,
now I'm not theirs to give, and they won't grieve.

I was so young, a girl-child, nothing more,
when I lay next to Mahlon in your home,
dreamt my future as his wife, the floor

beneath us humming with the wedding song,
and as the party danced into the morning,
I whispered to my husband *I belong*.

From the Norse

Stones and sand
tipped into my mouth
when I first spoke
your language.
How I gave myself away
as the wind blew
my vowels
into a new shape.

Gethsemane

At Easter you show me
your garden,
lead me down the paths
of hidden plants.

Only the tulips
stand upright,
black hearts
open at noon

as we catch
the nameless scent
that's woken
stumbling bees.

Later I'll trace
a path in muscle
and sinew
from shoulder to hip,

reading a map
of your vocation
under cover
of your skin,

while in the garden
the tulips blow
tight scarlet kisses
to the moon.

Washing Up

If you weren't expecting me
to kiss your neck, unseen
in the steam of the kitchen window,
you would feel that old rush of blood,
that blush as if you weren't past forty.
You'd turn and I'd hold you,
your marigolds sticking out sideways
like the arms of a scarecrow.

This has been our dance for years,
jigsaw fitting, two pieces of sky.
It's not about the surprise you say,
but knowing the steps, our tango,
danced and sung through the blue
of a decade or two.

Young Red and the Urban Fox

I won't start at the beginning of my story,
it was shit and way too long. I'll give you
the middle bit. The end isn't written yet.

I was a shadow player, puppeteering with two fingers
at passing cars, their headlights throwing a rabbit
against the old brick of the railway arch.

You'll want to know how I got suckered in.
Think me stupid? Lonely, hungry, empty, yes,
but this Riding Hood was nobody's fool,

until a fox in wolf's clothing, soft fur, browning grey
and tipped with silver, offered me the keys to his earth
and I, with nowhere else to go, smelled luxury.

Called me sweetie, stroked my pelt, showed me off
to all his foxy crew, cradled my limbs in his mouth
and, only when I struggled, sank his teeth into my bones,

stripped me to the skin. I'd like to say I did him in,
but this is not a fairy tale. He's out there still, prowling round
   the bins.
If you should see him, do me a favour – set your dog on him.

Seventeen

Remember me? I was the lad
who shouted loudest from the bus
at convent girls in tartan skirts,

threw burning matches up the front,
where new kids sat, gripping shiny
satchels on their laps. Yes, it was me

who planned to shag every slag
in school, get out, go south, be a punk
in a band in Camden Town, shack up

with a model in Chelsea. I was the boy
who'd make it big, bigger than you,
with your saddo dreams of nine to five.

Do you remember the night I drove my dad's
Rover into a wall, blood running thick
with alcohol? That's what happened to me.

Functional Skills Maths

If there are 4.5 litres in a gallon and
Gary's car does 52 miles to the gallon and
there's a petrol station 5 kilometres away,
where petrol is 2p per litre cheaper,
is it worth Gary making the extra journey?

When Gary pulls onto the ring-road
he senses a darker side,
beyond the edge of sodium town.
He knows the woods are waiting for him,
flicking stars between their fingertips.
He parks in a lay-by, leaves the car,
eyes wide to the deep, black heart of the wood,
and just like in a fairy tale,
he is never seen again.

You must show your workings, you must
explain assumptions used.
Values must be clearly stated.

Glassworks

That school trip, remember the girl
who waited her turn on the glassblower's pipe,
the one whose turn never came,

the one on her own on the bus
going home, the girl never picked
for school plays? She was the one

whose dad had the shop, who sat
all day on the countertop, fed with
Love Hearts and candy cigars.

She was the girl with the face
you could trust, learned accounts,
got a job, moved away,

creamed off the payroll, bought
a horse, bought a house,
a whole new life, you might say,

blew the hurt and the anger
into a ball, cooled the glass,
into something beautiful.

Now she waits every day
for the knock on the door,
for the glass to break,

for someone to take her away.

Poster Girl

This is how you see me,
just like the girl in the poster from the movie.
But I'm not her, never would have been
able to meet your eye like she can.

That actress, what's her name?
God! If only I'd had her chin,
her lovely clear skin, do you think
I'd have got myself into the mess I'm in?

And the boyfriend, the one she kills, he's nothing
like my man, even though they show him
knocking back the beers, knocking her for six,
he isn't half as fat and that's another thing

about a film, you can't smell his skin or her fear
and that's a shame if you ask me, and people do,
frequently – *what's it like to be in a movie?*
Well I don't know. I wasn't, was I?

I was in my life, with him. And it was shit.
That's why I took a knife
and cut and cut and cut
my sad way out of it.

Two boys 1963

Jack and I were ladies,
Autumn, a Lincolnshire fairground,
grand ladies with handbags
spun off the waltzers.

Jack was four,
I was five, a grown-up
stooped to his height,
best side to the camera,

smart in my blue jersey,
baggy trousers held up by braces,
shoved into Wellington boots.
I knew that ladies smiled,

Jack was made up with mud.
Uncle Joe's tripod slipped
on soft ground, business slow,
he captured us being ladies for the day.

Flea Bite

Black dots like fleas, folded in the sheets
of a delegate list, form a name I haven't seen
for thirty years. A quick bite and the itch begins.
At the tea break, I try not to look rattled
while across the room we both pretend
to engineer a moment of surprise.

Fancy seeing you here!
You introduce me as someone you studied
with and I want to say, *studied, don't you mean,
seduced?* It's a shame you haven't changed.
I'd find it easier if you were bald or grey.
I'd love to see the portrait in your attic, by the way.

All I can remember is you turned me
inside out and upside down, until my heart
was all over my sleeve and I wish that
I'd been cooler then. But now's my chance.
My teenage self wants to hurl hot tea
at your smirking grin and I can't help

wondering if you ever gave a fuck
and while I'm weighing up the words
I'll never say, I know I'm going to write
about this mixed-up thing I can't explain,
just like I did back then. And if you ever knew,
you'd still be smug about it, wouldn't you?

The End of the Affair

I cast for clues in the small waves that stroke
the harbour wall, as if the broken Picasso pieces
of your face can be hooked and reeled back in
slice by slice and re-assembled on the stones.

You throw a pebble and the shivering splash
sends your twisted smile to anchored yachts
that swing their painted hulls to a song
of masts, an orchestra of one-stringed harps.

When I turn to look at you, your eyes
are following the moon, as she slips
her moorings, floats to the harbour mouth
and sails out into the open sea.

Birth Certificate

Finsbury Town Hall,
the young and loving parents
sit with their new collection
of ten fingers, ten toes, a mouth, a nose,
all to be accounted for.

Advice given and ignored,
jokes made about jokey names,
and then out into the rain,
one drop falling on the baby
and one on the page,

a baptism of blurred ink.

The Axe Sings its Own Song

His great hand cleaves to my handle,
splitting the smaller logs,
cutting a shout in cold air,
rooks thrown to the clouds.

This is the real work, the work of weekends,
sharp air, blue sky, cotton cap, overalls.
Behind his eyes, a grey suit hangs
hated in the wardrobe.

In time, his grip grows age-soft.
I am given to his daughter's lover,
a dowry, cutting kindling to keep
a grandchild warm by the fire.

Late

for Isaac and Reuben

November tea-time,
he sits on his feet
in Ninja prayer.

Sometimes I stand outside,
shadow by the gate,
longing to shutter up the light show.

The other one smiles
his father's smile, my father's eyes,
pokes his brother in the back.

They stir, reply unheard,
and leave the stage.
It all goes on without me.

Isaac Plays the Part of the Sun

My son dances in orange and gold
carried high by a stronger boy
and there's such joy
that my heart swells
until my sternum splits
crack, crack
with the beauty of it
each leap
each hold
each lift.

Fenrir

He slips in before dawn, a shadow running with wolves.
That thatch of hair, once slicked wet over the fontanelle,
is hidden, hooded. Grey eyes, grown used to darkness,
catch and shine. I know the blood in his veins is mine.

Daylight. I watch him sleep, pale as death, then I retreat
over nests of underwear. Just before I close the door
on sour air, I gather up one huge shoe and feel again
the foot that hit my ribcage with its first fierce kick.

My Boy is Eighteen Today

He didn't die in the shallow waters of a Turkish beach.
He wasn't carried high on his father's shoulders
at the storming of the Macedonian border.
He won't sleep tonight in the subway beneath
Keleti station, nor will he run between cars
on the Calais motorway, or climb on the roof of a train.

Your boy will not see another birthday,
his suffering is over, his joy is over, his smile
is over. The bear he holds in the photo is over.
It keeps happening, over and over, on my screen,
in the water, on the road, on the rail track,
while my boy wakes, and turns eighteen today.

What can I say?

Hands

She casts on twenty stitches, a conjuring trick,
and leaves me sitting in the shade to knit.
My sticky summer fingers ache,
keeping time with my lips: *in, round,*
over, through. When one slips, I hold
on tight, run to find my grandmother
pacing among the raspberry canes,
long hands ready to catch and save.
Then she'll bend to show me how
to stroke the back of a bumblebee.

Grandmother

I open my eyes to sunlight
pouring through daffodil curtains,
a daffodil sun, the sound
of a cockerel, somewhere a cow.

She wakes downstairs in the limed-oak
bed from Barrow's Stores, where
her husband rose to be manager,
before cancer shrank him to nothing.

Now the city's behind her. She pounds
the earth, straight-backed, in size-eight shoes.
I run beside her as she walks the cracked,
yellow clay of the land back into her bones.

1974

Dad's brass lighter rides
bareback on green onyx,
around a matching ashtray island.

On best behaviour, I spy
Players No.6 tucked
behind the coaster stand.

Liberal Party Wine and Cheese,
Hirondelle and Primula,
young men flutter round my mum

but one cool couple stands apart,
He's an architect and she's such fun.
Pinstripe flares loom up from Cuban heels,

she flies, floral cotton, in the face
of all those perms. Frieda and Malcolm.
I wish they were my Dad and Mum.

When backs are turned, my brother and I
swig dregs of red, till howls tear the air
of the cocktail hour and blood runs thick

from a rock-shaped wound on his brow.
Onyx and brass still in my hand,
no chance of being adopted now.

Unreliable Memoir

I

I can still remember,
when I was four,
the day the boat
got stuck on a rock,
swung like a drunk
till a bikini-clad
Diana Rigg jumped in
and pulled us ashore.
We were so sure it was
really her, we forgot
to be afraid.

II

I can almost remember
being fifteen, when
no-one understood,
except Darren O'Hare
from down the road
who had a weird way
of showing it, showed it
in fact by the derelict house
and I laughed,
though really
I felt sick.

III

I'll always remember
the night of the bombs,
Mulberry Tree, Tavern in the Town,
my parents at a concert
in the old Town Hall. I heard
the howl of sirens merge and split
away along the Bristol Road.
Now I lie awake,
the same prayer on my lips,
every time my sons
are late coming home.

Sunday Afternoon

Uneven knuckles tighten as he grips the tray,
silver spoons play on bone china cups. She leans

against the sagging arm of the settee, feet up, watches
racing on TV, follows Willie Carson riding Little Wolf.

Tissue-paper skin traps years beneath her chins.
She loosens her stays, softens, fills the space.

He clears his throat, she doesn't hear. He pours, stirs,
hands her the cup, its saucer settles in her lap.

And I am there, sitting on the stool beside the fire
perhaps, or underneath the table with the spaniel,

unseen or heard, watching dust glitter and twist
in the light which hangs between them, waiting

for the sign it's time – the dog's tail thumping
on the floor, the old man's hand in pocket,

keys jingling, last drop of tea swallowed, horses
a blur of colour – for the dog and I to slip out

into cool air, jump and circle one other, while he
leans on his stick, filmy blue eyes watering.

The Night My Father Died

I stepped outside, to a sky pierced with light,
as if each star was begging me to believe
in an afterlife, and each stab of brightness
was a window for looking down on the living.
I wished on the brightest star that it was true,
knowing, but choosing to forget, that he wouldn't
have had any truck with that, he would have said
death is death and that is all there is.
But, noticing a star I hadn't seen before,
above the next door factory wall, hanging
like new against the winter sky, I couldn't help
but whisper up to it: *goodnight Dad. Goodbye.*

The Message

Hello Mum, it's me.
I thought you'd be back by now.
I hope it went okay, so
I suppose it must have done,
although, if you're still there

then perhaps they've kept you in.
I'm waffling now, sorry,
tell you what, I'll ring again
tomorrow, or, if you get in,
ring me, right?

I'm sure you're fine
and if you're not
they'll tell me, won't they?
You did remember, didn't you,
to give my name, as next of kin?

Portmeirion

Like falling into the half-waking
dream of a man-child, every colour
in the paint-box laid thick
over a world with its own rules.
A presidential doll's house tucked
into the cliffs, fuchsia pink, stunted,
in a land of giants and dwarves.

Hindu gods and goddesses dance
on pillars, children shriek
through the fountain. Venus
and the saints sleep in alcoves
of lapis blue. Warped angles,
elliptical windows, pantile roofs,
lead me up winding paths

until, through a slantways gap, I see
mountains, the estuary, heathland
against a muted, watercolour sky
and I think of you here, Dad, on holiday
with Mum, one of those summers
when we'd all left home.
Weird, you would have said.

And weird enough to imagine
I might see you now, if I just
turn fast enough, stooping
under an impossible arch,
straightening to take it in, while Mum
buys a bowl from the gift shop,
and you smile, shake your head.

Omen

Driving our parents'
too-large car,
like a child in a dream,
as if I'd never learned,
I came to find you,
my brother,
in the dark
on the edge of town.

As I swung wildly
round a corner,
where black hedges
nudged the lane,
a sudden owl flew,
and I knew, I knew.

Inquest

A thin man, my brother slips between the pages.
It was all in the details: a note to spare the chambermaid
and the longest thing he ever wrote, a letter to his wife.

The contents of the bin, they kept, gave them to her
six months later – sweet wrappers, she gave them back.
They said the sheets were slept in. What did he dream?

Did he remember when we sat on a rock in Kodacolour?
Who was the king? I climbed up to see, he climbed to jump.
Sewn together in secret, I lost him first when I was nine,

kept a shrine in the summerhouse till the leaves blew in.
I thought the stitches would dissolve in time,
but now I trace a broken line, where I have lost a limb.

Collecting Reuben From School

my grandfather told me
that rain was God's tears of joy

Now I wrap
the blackest wool
around my head,
against the driving snow.

Boots pound packed ice,
hurry down the short cut,
hedges hacked back,
nests of brambles soft
under cold covers.

I promise I'll be there

In the playground
you wrap yourself around me,
for now we know
flesh and blood can die away.

The landscape
can change
overnight.

On Burgess Street

Though you are gone
I see your face in the street,
your walk, and the long
flow of your coat, the angle of your feet.

I see your face in the street,
my heart, for one moment, leaps
for the flow of your coat, angle of your feet,
the mind is tricked and reason sleeps.

My heart, for one moment leaps
for the hat that covered thinning hair,
the mind is tricked and reason sleeps,
I know, but cannot bear

the hat that covered thinning hair
is not your hat, is not your head,
I know but cannot bear
to speak the word, all words are dead.

It's not your hat, it's not your head!
My mouth begins to make your name,
to speak the word, all words are dead.
Your hair, your height, your shape, your frame,

my mouth begins to make your name,
the stranger turns – I hold my breath,
your hair, your height, your shape, your frame,
the face has changed, as if in death.

The stranger turns, I hold my breath,
but your walk and your long
face have changed
and you are gone.

In the Burrows of the Nightmare

i.m. D.P.C . 1962 – 2005

There's a faceless congregation
who ask for you by name,
claim they do not know what happened,

they try to make me speak,
but my mouth is full of sleep,
I have no liturgy.

Our father, who is in heaven,
slips in and sits down
in an almost-familiar room

where the furniture is oddly stacked,
jumbled against us,
he did not live to see you

pack your bags
and dance your moonlit dance,
your moonlit flit.

The room is full
of father, son and holy ghosts,
and when they ask for you again, I pray

bring me the sounds of morning,
to milk-bottle-clatter me awake.

Without You On the Beach at Rhosneigr

As children, you and I would wonder at
the seventh wave, the big one with the power
to move the whole sea further in or out,
and counting on our hands, we'd map the hour
and multiply by twelve, till we got stuck
in working out high-tide or low and when
or where the seaweed line would form, and luck
was in that wave, and we were lucky then.
Now tear-salt stings my skin, I stand alone
in shallow water, measuring the fall and rise
of all those little waves, until that one
familiar surge, from somewhere deep inside,
howls out to God the cursing grief of years
– and no-one but an oyster catcher hears.

Fog

Earth-sweat, sea-breath
hangs about, cold-shouldering street corners,
disconsolate, untouchable,
smothers horizons, pockets whole villages,
sprays dirty thumb-smudge graffiti
on city walls, in ditches,
spits chill onto the woollen scarves of citizens,
who shrink into their coats, avert their gaze

until cloud-fall sighs and heaves itself away
– a slow unfathomable fade –
to hide in low valleys and the shadows of churches,
waiting to muster when the day's back turns.

Praise Poem for the Sea

I write in praise of the suck
and undertow of waves on shingle,

I write in praise of the grey-green
merge of water into sky,

I write in praise of its iron will, its urge
to drag and pull every small thing in.

I write in praise of its kissing
and tangling love for the wind,

of its teeth carving out caves
and hacking into cliffs. I write

in praise of the sea and the songs
of gulls, terns, kittiwakes, fisherman

and sailors' wives keening unheeded.

I write in praise of it leaving me, stripped
to the bone, by the outgoing tide, polished,

transfixed, just another white stone.
I write until the paper blows away,

the pencil breaks, my hair whips
across my face – like a torn plastic bag

on a driftwood branch, my salt-cracked
lips split, my voice lost to the wind.

Smokers

for the actors of Theatre Day Productions, Gaza

In the shelter of a café on the other side,
November sunshine warming us, we sit
touching hands as worlds collide.

I hear the story of your friends who died.
Our fingers brush, your cigarette is lit,
in the shelter of a café on the other side.

The Surgeon General warns us: *Smoking is Suicide.*
You gave up giving up when bullets hit.
Touching hands as worlds collide,

you talk of family, home and what's implied
by loss of hope and all that's lost with it,
in the shelter of a café on the other side.

We shake our heads at nations that divide
their land, tear the heart from skin that's split,
touching hands as worlds collide.

I want to hold your pain and let it slide
inside my soul, but that's too intimate
in the shelter of a café on the other side,
touching hands as worlds collide.

Senseless Act of Violence

i.m. Jo Cox 1974-2016

Something about the London air
thick with the sour breath of taxis,
vans and back-alley smokers,

the sky black, the news blacker,
made me fear the Underground,
the bus, busy streets, public places.

I chose to walk instead, my heart
and lungs yearning for a breeze,
to throw off the sense of dread.

Inside, we held our meeting, cooled
by an air-conditioned hum, lulled
for a moment, forgetting our fear

until the door opened and our friend
stepped in. *It's Jo Cox,* she said,
Brendan's wife, there's been a shooting.

Not here but there, a northern place,
a town square by a library
where you never would expect it.

That afternoon, walking back to Kings Cross,
I hung on the news, signal to signal, until
the text came – *Jo Cox is dead* –

and finally, it rained.

Marie Colvin

Driving home I hear on the radio

> *the news has just come in*

a name I feel I know

> *only yesterday she was on the BBC*

but it's not your voice

> *speaking about a baby hit by shell-fire*

just coincidence, the surname

> *his chest heaving and then not heaving.*

so why do I find myself crying?

> *A man described as a freedom fighter*

I stop the car

> *says:* we will name our streets for her

Tsunami, Boxing Day 2004

Dunstanburgh, the children point out
a seal on the beach, rotted and oozing,
fly-covered, slick black slug, washed high
among the matchstick wood.

Wind blows rain in our eyes
until we turn away, while on TV
every channel carries news
of bodies bloated by an ocean,

a shred, a remnant of cloth hooked
to a splinter of someone's house.
I carry my tears around my solid home,
hold my children too tight.

The Visit

When she phoned, she said you were outside
watching a bat track its nightly flight-path
between shed and porch, playing a solo,
call and response, always the same trajectory.

We had to work it, she and I, like the weave
of the log basket; in and out, to seem
like it was your idea. We held you easily
between us, your old weight desiccated.

In time, you let me in and we sat
in the conservatory, listening to the trapped
buzz of a bumblebee, while rabbits invaded
the polytunnel, ragwort spread in the veg patch.

But at least the grass is cut, you said,
at least I've managed that.

Today They Buried His Wife

Telly off, he stares at its blankness,
forgets the tea in the pot,
marshy and cooling, dark as old blood.

There's topsoil under his nails
from that last handful of earth,
and he can still taste the ham

slipping between teeth and gum.
The grave is six foot by three,
rich, heavy soil, well-drained,

perfect for courgettes, purple beans,
a weeping cherry to lie beneath,
chat to her, with a smoke and a beer.

Between headstones and plastic pots,
he'll make a garden grow; away
from this room, where the dark shape

of her chair recalls how her body
cultivated death, and the air
still hangs with her last breath.

Gloria

She was the lady who lived on trains.
Greeted each day by the push-button
smile of the toilet door, she'd finessed

the art of stripping and washing
in the metal sink. She'd an eye
for the seat where views were best,

booked ahead to save on rent
and the plotting of daughters
who would put her away.

The south coast to Edinburgh,
on to Inverness, a stretch
of her legs, then back again.

Once or twice, if a train was delayed,
a guard would offer her a taxi home.
My son will pick me up, she said,

he's good like that, kind to his mum.
Keith, she called him, sometimes John.
A name she could rely on.

Sestina for Rachel

Sunday afternoon, her grandparents' home,
a child escapes from grown-up talk to the packed snow,
double-paged spread, of a National Geographic photo
essay — *the Inuit diet is of fish,*
caught through the ice, hook and line dropped in water,
families sleep in their igloo, wrapped in the warmth

of caribou skins. Here, the fires are lit, warmth
of late sun on red sandstone, the cows crowd home
at four o'clock, duckweed settles on the trout pond;
in a month or two there may be snow
and she'll revel in its novelty, while the Inuit child watches fish
circle for eternity beneath the ice hole in the photo.

The old and the young gather for a photo
in the farmhouse, appearing like ghosts in the warmth
of Polaroid burgundy, brown and red of fish
buttons on her ribbed acrylic cardigan. Then home
to the city; her fingers feel the folded page in her skirt pocket,
 the snow
spread across that other child's black and white world, as water

runs down the car window like tadpoles, the water
of old tears mixing with new rain. Her mother will place the
 new photo
in the album, her own Geographic, next to last winter's
Shovelling Snow
at the Farm, while the Inuit child curls up with her family in the
 warmth
of furs trapped by a father, who wraps up his daughter in her
 icy home.
Caribou, igloo, seal skin, raw fish,

chips, formica, lawnmower, goldfish
circling their bowl, peering at themselves through water,
dark from neglect. Mother and daughter in an empty home,
watched from the mantelpiece by a photo
from before, the warmth
of a smile that makes unthinkable this drifting snow

that settles in their mouths, this snow
which threatens to bury them. And still the child waits for the
    fish,
the grandparents hold out their hands to the warmth
of the fire and the fat brown trout stirs in the water,
beneath the duckweed, safe from rod and hook, home
in cloudy mud, until colour fades from the Polaroid photo.

Long ago, in a home where warmth
melted snow to water,
was a photo of a man with his daughter, lifting high a great
    brown fish.

Made in Bradford

In Drummond's Mill
the weaving shed is empty,
the ghosts hold their breath.
I see a different room,
broad and still,
pillars holding a vaulted ceiling,
the Mosque at Cordoba,
vast expanse of empty floor,
where once another congregation
knelt and wove their prayers.

Ghandi

Darwen, Lancashire, 1931

I

Mary Judson – weaver

If I could, I'd press him
to my big bosom,

tight as the one I lost,
the same bald head,

shrunken limbs swaddled.
I'd have him in my arms,

hold him till the life
came back.

Constable Frederick Clarkson

I was holding back the women,
surging forward, not with anger,
but with love. A great crush of it.

Let their men see they love a gentle man,
I've had enough of calling
through letterboxes, hammering on doors.

This uniform, each button
like a tiny shield, too small
to shelter even him.

III

Kathleen Jebb – aged five

A great crowd
of tree-trunk legs,
stockings and boots

and one pair naked,
sandaled and wrapped
above the knee

in white, like it says
in the Bible,
and I got close enough to touch,

felt his hand on my head,
a blessing like spun gold,
candyfloss, pure light,

and hands pulled me up,
raised me to shoulder height,
and now when I look

at the photograph from the paper,
it makes no sense,
all that grey. That rain.

Councillor Bestwick

My duty was to welcome him,
little peasant, hushing our looms,
wishing we were brothers.

My suit was pinstripe woollen worsted,
he could keep his homespun,
take it back where he came from.

He looked at me and knew I'd fought a war,
battled hand to hand and held another man
face down, drowned him in a pool of clay.

Like a blackbird on the guttering,
singing two notes, the Indian's sharp eyes
caught me in my shame.

Five Haiku

*after Benjamin West's 'Alexander III of Scotland Rescued from the Fury of a Stag by the intrepidity of Colin Fitzgerald':
National Galleries of Scotland*

I

Away home for your
tea, Colin. Stop showing off
now, no-one's watching.

II

Last night I googled
your name to see. Largs '63,
remember me?

III

I stole a feather
from your cap, side by side
in Miss Mackenzie's class.

IV

Pink suits you. You've put
on weight, there's colour in your
cheeks. Do you work out?

V

Now that I've found you,
Colin Fitzgerald, I will
never let you go.

The Wrong Label

The Christmas I unwrapped an Eagle annual
there was Dan Dare, all black lines, strong jaw,
the Mekon, slime-green, repulsive, sucking me in.
Each comic strip a rush of danger, thrill of speed.

Minutes in to this new-found joy, a cry went up,
my brother sat with a Twinkle annual in his lap.
I fought my case, ruined Christmas with my argument,
and lost. *These things happen, simple mistake.*

I flicked the pages of Twinkle, where fat-faced
children smiled pink-lipped smiles, cherubic.
I was having none of it. I spent the afternoon
plotting how to make the Eagle mine.

The Gift

A green plastic plane drops from my cracker
onto the plate and I make myself tiny, climb aboard.
Nobody sees. They go on talking, drinking, arguing
over the Rights of Kings, turkey or goose,
deaths of celebrities and whether this year
was worse than any other, or is it a matter of perception?

While I grip my green plastic carry-on bag,
sit back in my seat, let a green plastic pilot
fly me away to a place where the weather might turn
and I'll be forced to stay, snowed in, alone,
in a cottage by the sea, just me,
watching the water and the sky.

Czechoslovakia

after Miroslav Holub

Go and open the door
and maybe you'll see
the small white house,
the country house of his father,
where he drew water from the spring
and washed your hair in a jug
as you lay on your back
on the bench in the yard.

Go and open the door
and you'll see the castle
high on the fairytale hill,
surrounded by larches in bud.
Remember how you asked him
if a princess lived there?
And how surprised you were
to learn it was an asylum.

Go and open the door
and maybe you'll see
the castle is empty,
its prisoners are among us.

Distance

for Julia Chitrakar

My city is like
a model village,
where I half expect
the giant face
of a child to peer in
at my café window
or a huge foot
to crush the tourists,
walking like ants
on the walls.

Your city is like
a pan of spices
frying on a hot stove
in a kitchen
whose back door opens
behind the Durbar Square,
mustard seeds popping
like tiny explosions
and smoke,
always smoke,
in the air.

We look up
at different skies,
where your eagles,
my seagulls,
wheel in and out of view.
We step inside
our shopping malls
and you buy
the watch I wear,
while I buy the DVD
you watched last Sunday
with your boys.

Burial Goods

Hand in earth, pressing home a tulip bulb,
I feel glass, guess a bottle, count your sides,
name you hexagon, hold you to the light,
see through you to a dark back room;
white antimacassars, curtains half-closed.

Indoors, washed clean, you smell of nothing
and I wonder what you held. Something sweet?
Eau de violet dabbed on a cheek,
or ink to write letters to the Front?

I put you on the mantelpiece,
that same marble slab
where once a telegram stood,
and I wait for the morning sun
to pour through your clear blue skin.

Secondary, 2017

I. HOPE

after Emily Dickinson

My pillow is the thing with feathers,
sheet crisp as frosted snow.
Outside my window
a gull floats,
white kite on a taut string
rising on a thermal.

II. HOSPITAL SONG

The other women breathe the heavy breath
of sleepers with few nights left to sleep.

I plug my headphones in. Give me a mix
of Dolly, her candyfloss hairdo, her smile.

Give me 'The Games People Play',
'Nine to Five' and 'I Will Always Love You'.

When I'm home, I'll wake to the throat-song
of wood pigeons singing the same notes

I heard as a child, shrugging off night fears
as I open my eyes to the light.

III. ELEGY IN DUST

I search in the Thesaurus for a synonym for dust, and as I am about to shut the book, a tiny spider walks across the page: a motion once begun cannot easily be undone, the spider is crushed against the words, *Dies Irae...*

I will show you all the sights and smells of the island: here's the knife shop with its meat cleavers, hunting weapons, sickles with curlicue ram's horn tails and beyond the darkened doorway, do you see? The cutler stands, curved belly and glasses, stirring the boiling pan. He renders sheep's bones for handles and drowns the chamomile air, which rises underfoot over dips and mounds of land wrapped in dusty olive trees.

And when I look up, the fog has swallowed the world I knew. Only a lick of flat water leads over damp, green fields. A mirror glass path, a Stygian canal to the sea. Yesterday you asked me: mother, where will we bury you? And I told you. Take a boat through the harbour rocks and halfway to the middle rocks, that are called Starvation, throw my ashes into the waves, where I threw my father's and watched his dust cloud blow and settle, the grit sinking before the powder.

IV. RELIC

Once this hand held my father's,
stroked warmth into fingers
pinched cold by Raynaud's.

Today this hand touches hard skins
of Conference pears to see if they will soften,
or turn black before they can ripen.

One day this hand will struggle to write
about fathers and fruit, and when it stops,
you can tuck it away in a box, along with rest of me

and put it under the pear tree.

Ceremony

Clear away the dead wood and feed the hungry fire
with every dragged branch, half-rotten log,
handful of leaves within your reach.

Twist and bend, dancing that ancient forgotten thing,
hands in gloves, sodden and chilling. Pause to drink
tea from the flask, eat Christmas cake, eat fast.

Then turn, catch cloudy breath just long enough
to see the clearing grow. Watch flames swallow
brushwood, breathe out tongues that shiver up to sky.

Work on until the fat moon rises low and calls time
on the day. Only now can you walk away,
into the cool dark, while fire burns out its heart.

You may return when charred ground is rain-soft,
pace the earth and count the space each tree
will need to thrive. Now dig the holes and plant.

The Dance

In the dream
I am younger,
the room is huge
and I dance
over a wooden floor.
I do it often. It's what I do.
I have a huge room,
as high as a church,
to myself and I dance across
its beautiful wooden floor
again and again.

When I wake
the dance is still in me.
It lightens my limbs,
moves me to the kitchen.
The coffee brews on the hob
and I dance back and forth
from the table
to the fridge
and I am young
again and again.